DATE DUE		11-30
FEB. 1 8	NOV. 0 8 MAR 26	
MAR. 1 8	NOV. 1 5	2-8
APR. 0 6	OCT. 2	10-11
APR. 2 7	OCT. 3 1	12-6
FEB. 0 9	DEC. 1 9	3-7
MAR. 1 5	APR. 3 0	0-3
APR. 2 6	DEC. 1 5	11-2
OCT. 0 4	OCT. 0 5	1-23
APR. 0 4	MAR. 8	2-27
	Sept 2	4-6
		4-26

4344

Weiss, Monica
 Birthday cake
 candles,
  counting

Birthday Cake Candles
Counting

Written by Monica Weiss
Illustrated by Rose Mary Berlin

Troll Associates

Library of Congress Cataloging-in-Publication Data

Weiss, Monica.
     Birthday cake candles, counting / by Monica Weiss; illustrated by
Rose Mary Berlin.
          p.   cm.—(Frimble family first learning adventures)
     Summary: Photographs of Mr. Frimble's first nine birthdays
demonstrate how he learned to get along with his sister.
     ISBN 0-8167-2496-2 (lib. bdg.)   ISBN 0-8167-2497-0 (pbk.)
     [1. Brothers and sisters—Fiction.   2. Birthdays—Fiction.
3. Family life—Fiction.   4. Frogs—Fiction.   5. Counting.]
I. Berlin, Rose Mary, ill.   II. Title.   III. Series: Weiss, Monica.
Frimble family first learning adventures.
PZ7.W448145Bi   1992
[E]—dc20   91-16033

Published by Troll Associates.

Copyright © 1992 by GRAYMONT ENTERPRISES, Inc.
Printed in the United States of America.
10   9   8   7   6   5   4   3   2   1

Charlie and Anna were fighting.
"Hold on, kids!" Mr. Frimble said.
"Anna always teases me," said Charlie.
"Charlie always bothers me," Anna said.
"I wish I didn't have a brother!" said Anna.
"I wish I didn't have a sister!" said Charlie.

3

"Hmm," smiled Mr. Frimble. "Sometimes it's hard to get along. But you'll see, things get easier as you get older."

Mr. Frimble took a big photo album from the shelf.

"Let me show you this," he said.

He opened the album.

Mr. Frimble showed Charlie and Anna the first picture.

"Here's a picture of me when I was one year old, my very first birthday. See? There's one candle on the cake. There's one balloon and there's one present.

"...And I thought I had that whole cake to *myself*," he said.

Mr. Frimble turned to the second page. "Here's my second birthday party. Two candles, two balloons, two of us.

"But my older sister Pam made it clear that she wanted a piece of the cake, too."

"Then I was three. There were three
candles, three balloons, and three of us.
I opened my presents, and my mama said
I had to share."

11

Mr. Frimble pointed to the next picture in the album.

"Here's a picture of me when I was four," he said.

"Four candles, four balloons, and a fine family of four: my mama, my papa, my sister Pam, and me.

" 'Four is a fine time for making friends,' my papa said to us."

13

"When I was five, my Grandpa Sid came to my birthday party. There were five candles and five balloons, one for each person at the party.

"Grandpa gave me a book. He gave one to Pam, too. He told us we were old enough to share ideas."

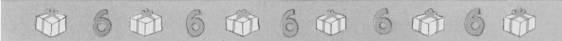

"On my sixth birthday, there were six of us at my party. I dropped a piece of cake on Aunt Betty's lap. Pam giggled and I was very embarrassed."

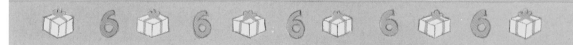

"The next year, when I was seven, Uncle Bert dropped a piece of cake in his own lap.

"Pam giggled and so did I. I bet old Bert was pretty embarrassed.

"Everything was seven: seven candles, seven balloons, and seven Frimbles."

Mr. Frimble turned to the next page.
"So then I was eight. I let Pam help me blow out the candles. We were beginning to like each other a little better."

"And here's a picture of my ninth birthday. Pam made my birthday cake herself! I guess we were starting to realize what my parents had said all along—that brothers and sisters could be good friends."

"We've looked at enough of my old pictures," said Mr. Frimble. "As you can see, things worked out for me and my sister. And they'll work out for you too."

Anna took her brother's hand. "Come on, Charlie, let's go play," she said.

"Okay, okay," said Charlie, "but only if you stop teasing me."

"All right, all right," Anna said, "but only if you stop bothering me."

24